JONI'S STORY

Books in the Today's Heroes Series

JONI'S STORY

by Joni Eareckson Tada
with Joe Musser
and Linda Lee Maifair

ZondervanPublishingHouse

Grand Rapids, Michigan

A Division of HarperCollinsPublishers

Joni's Story
Abridged from the books *Joni* and *Choices, Changes*
Joni copyright © 1976 by Joni Eareckson and Joe Musser
Choices, Changes copyright © 1986 by Joni Eareckson Tada
Abridgment copyright © 1992 by Zondervan Publishing House

Requests for information should be addressed to:
Zondervan Publishing House
Grand Rapids, Michigan 49530

Library of Congress Cataloging-in-Publication Data

Tada, Joni Eareckson.
    Joni's Story / by Joni Eareckson Tada.
        p.   cm.
    Summary: The author describes how her faith in God was
challenged after a diving accident left her paralyzed at
the age of seventeen.
    ISBN 0-310-58661-5 (paper)
    1. Tada, Joni Eareckson—Health—Juvenile literature. 2. Quad-
riplegics—United States—Biography—Juvenile literature.
3. Christian life—Juvenile literature. [1. Tada, Joni Eareckson.
2. Quadriplegics. 3. Physically handicapped. 4. Christian life.]
I. Title.
RC406.P3T33   1992
362.4'3'092—dc20
[B]   92–14690
                                                                    CIP
                                                                     AC

Abridged by Linda Lee Maifair
Edited by Bruce and Becky Durost Fish
Interior designed by Rachel Hostetter
Interior illustrations by Gloria Oostema
Cover designed by Mark Veldheer
Cover illustration by Patrick Kelley

Printed in the United States of America

97 / LP / 10 9 8

CONTENTS

Chronology of Events

1950. Joni is born in Baltimore, Maryland.

July 30, 1967. At age seventeen, Joni breaks her neck in a diving accident.

1969. Joni returns home and begins taking speech classes at the University of Maryland.

1970. Joni meets Donald Bertolli.

1973. Baltimore celebrates Joni Eareckson Day; Joni begins Joni PTL.

1974. Joni appears on the "Today" show and begins writing her autobiography.

1978. World Wide Pictures makes a movie of the book *Joni.*

1979. Joni begins Joni and Friends, a ministry with the handicapped.

1982. Joni marries Ken Tada.

1

The Moment Everything Changed

Humming softly, I saddled Tumbleweed and swung up to mount her. It was a beautiful day with warm sunshine and gentle breezes. It was good to be out of the city.

I pressed my thighs against Tumbleweed's sides and nudged her with my heels. The mare headed up the dusty road at a walk. When we came to the pasture, I dug my heels again. Tumbleweed didn't need coaxing. She loved to run as much as I loved to ride. We flew across the field, the wind in my hair.

Tumbleweed cantered toward the first practice jump. I tightened my knees against her body. We lifted up and over the fence. It was exciting to soar nearly ten feet in the air. We were both good jumpers. We had won all kinds of ribbons and horse show awards.

After several good runs around the course, Tumbleweed was wet with sweaty lather. I slowed her to a trot and turned back toward the barn.

Dad met me part way. Smiling, he reined in his big gray gelding. "I saw her jump, Joni," Dad said proudly. "She's in great shape. I think you'll run away with the ribbons at next week's show!"

It was the summer of 1967. The summer after I graduated from Woodlawn Senior High School. I had every reason to be happy and more than the horse show ribbons to look forward to.

I had a close, loving family: Mom and Dad and my sisters Jay, Kathy, and Linda. We enjoyed doing things together. We traveled out West, went on trail rides, camped in the hills, and attended church.

I had a boyfriend, Dick. He was tall and good-looking. A bit shy, Dick was a sensitive, mature Christian boy. We cared a lot about each other.

I was healthy and athletic. I had even been named captain of my high school lacrosse team. It had meant more to me than my nomination to the honor society.

I had good friends at school and in our

Christian youth club, Young Life. I enjoyed doing all the things teenagers like to do. I played the guitar. I sang. I went out on dates, worrying about what to wear and how to fix my hair. In the fall I would be going away to college.

I was happy, and I was grateful for all the good things God had given me. But deep inside I knew I wasn't the sort of person God expected me to be. I hadn't done as well as I could have in high school. Sometimes I fought with my parents. I had no real goals, no idea of what I wanted to do with my life. And no matter how hard I tried to improve, I kept giving in to my emotions. I was jealous. I got angry.

One day I prayed for things to change. "Lord," I insisted, "if you're really there, do something in my life that will change me. Do something that will turn me around. I want you to work in my life for real. I don't know how. But I'm begging you, Lord. Please do something in my life to turn it around."

Not long after that, I went swimming with my sister Kathy. The hot July sun was setting. The cool waters of the Chesapeake Bay glowed a warm red. It was a perfect day for swimming. I loved to swim, and I loved to dive.

I swam out, away from the others, to a small wooden raft and pulled myself up out of the water. I shook myself off, then balanced on the edge of the raft, my arms over my head.

I dived. The clean coldness of the water

doused my skin as my body broke the surface. It was the last thing my legs and arms would feel. Nothing in my life would ever be the same again.

2

At the Hospital

Everything happened at once. My head struck something hard. My body sprawled out of control. I heard a loud buzzing and felt a vibration, like an electric shock.

The next thing I knew, I was lying face down on the bottom. *How did I get here?* I wondered. *Why were my arms tied to my chest? Was I caught in something? A fishnet?* I tried to kick. I couldn't move my legs. *My feet must be caught too.*

I tried with all my strength to break free. Nothing happened. Still lying face down under the water, I could feel the pressure of holding my breath. I knew I couldn't hold it much longer. I was drowning. I couldn't move, and I couldn't call for help. My thoughts screamed in my head. *Help me! I don't want to die!*

"Joni! Joni!" I could hear my sister calling. I had no way to let her know I was in trouble. *Help me, Kathy. I'm stuck!*

The current lifted me up and let me down again. I settled back on the bottom. Broken shells and stones scraped my face and shoulders. The sand gritted against my chin and forehead.

"Joni, are you looking for shells?" Kathy asked. *Grab me! I can't hold my breath any longer!*

"Did you dive in here?" my sister asked. "It's so shallow."

I could see Kathy's shadow above me, but I couldn't move. I was out of air. Everything was going dark. *Oh, please, dear God. Don't let me die!*

I felt Kathy's arms around my shoulders. She tried to lift me. She stumbled, then lifted me again. Just before I fainted, my head came out of the water. Choking and gagging, I gulped in mouthfuls of air.

"Oh, thank you, God!" I said.

"Hey, are you okay?" Kathy asked.

I wasn't okay. I was confused and afraid. My arm still felt as if it were tied to my chest, but I could see it now, slung over Kathy's shoulder. None of my limbs were tied. My arms and legs dangled in the water, but I couldn't move them. Why?

Kathy called for help. Another swimmer helped

her lift me onto an inflated raft. They pushed me toward the shore. I tried to get up. My legs and arms refused to work. I felt like I was pinned against the raft. A crowd gathered around me, staring and whispering.

I was embarrassed. "Kathy, please make them leave," I said.

Kathy asked the people to move back. She told someone to call an ambulance.

"Kathy, I can't move!" I said. "Hold me!"

"I am, Joni." She lifted my hands to show me that she was holding them tightly.

I was more confused, more scared than before. "I can't feel it," I told her. "Squeeze me."

Kathy bent over and held me close. I couldn't feel her hug. "I don't feel that, either," I told her.

I could see the worry in her eyes. She touched my leg. "Can you feel this?"

"No," I said.

"This?" She squeezed my forearm.

"No!" I cried. "I can't feel it!"

Kathy tried to keep her voice calm. "How about this?" Her hand slid from my arm to my shoulder.

"Yes! Yes, I can feel that!"

We were both relieved. At last, somewhere on my body, I could feel something. I lay back on the raft and tried to make sense of what was happening. I knew I had hit my head when I dived into the water. The water must have been shallower than I thought. I must have injured something. That's why I was numb. I wondered how long it would last.

"Don't worry," I told my sister. "The Lord won't let anything happen to me. I'll be all right."

I heard the wail of a siren. An ambulance pulled up, and its doors opened. The attendants lifted me onto a stretcher and placed me in the back of the ambulance. Kathy climbed up behind me. The siren wailed again as we headed away from the beach.

"I hate to put you to all this trouble," I told the ambulance attendant. "Once I catch my breath, I'll be okay. The numbness will wear off soon." It had to be true.

The attendant didn't say anything. He reached over and brushed some sand off my face. Then he smiled and looked away. I wished he would tell me that I was going to be all right.

By the time we pulled up to the hospital emergency entrance, the sun had set. The sky was dark. I wanted to go home.

I was taken into the emergency room and put on a hospital table. The overhead lights hurt my eyes. The equipment—bottles, scissors, scalpels—frightened me. The antiseptic hospital smell made me queasy.

A nurse strapped me to the table and wheeled me into a small cubicle. I tried desperately to move my arms and legs while she pulled the curtains around my table. Tears welled up in my eyes. I felt so helpless. And scared.

"Can't you tell me what's happening to me?" I begged.

The nurse just shrugged and began taking off my rings. "The doctor will be here soon. I'm going to put your jewelry in this envelope. Regulations," she said.

"How long do I have to stay here? Can I go home tonight?" I asked.

Her voice was flat and emotionless. It reminded me of a telephone recording. "I'm sorry. You'll have to ask the doctor. Regulations."

She put the envelope on a nearby table. Then she opened a drawer and pulled out a big pair of shears. She stood by my table, the scissors in her hand.

"Wh—what are you going to do?" I asked.

"I've got to remove your swimsuit," she said.

"Don't cut it!" I begged her. "I just got it, and it's my fav—"

She didn't let me finish. "Sorry. Regulations," she said.

I could hear the clipping of the shears. Ch-cluck. Ch-cluck. Ch-cluck. She pulled off the ruined scraps of material and dropped what was left of my swimsuit in a waste can. I wanted to cry.

The nurse pulled a sheet up over me and left. The sheet slipped down, but I couldn't do anything about it. I whispered pieces of the Twenty-third Psalm. I tried to keep my mind off where I was and what was happening to me. I thought about Mom and Dad and my boyfriend, Dick. Had anybody told them yet?

A man in a white lab coat pulled back the curtain. "I'm Dr. Sherrill." He flipped through the papers on his clipboard. "And your name is Joanie?"

"It's pronounced Johnny," I told him. "I'm named after my father."

"Okay, Joni," the doctor said. "Let's see what happened to you."

"When can I go home?" I asked him. I had been there too long already.

He didn't answer. He pricked my feet and legs with a long pin. "Do you feel this, Joni?"

"No. I can't feel that." I wished he would tell me what it meant.

"How about this?"

I shut my eyes, trying to concentrate, hoping to feel something. "Nothing."

He held my arm and pressed the pin against my fingers. My wrist. My forearm. *Why can't I feel anything?* He touched my upper arm. Finally I felt a small sting in my shoulder.

"I feel that," I told him. "I had feeling there at the beach, too."

Dr. Sherrill wrote something on his clipboard.

Other medical staff appeared. Another doctor came over and watched while Dr. Sherrill went through the pin routine again. The only place I felt the pin pricks was in my shoulder.

"Looks like a fracture-dislocation," the doctors agreed. I didn't know what that meant. I only knew how scared I was and how much I wanted to go home.

Someone wiped my arm with a cotton ball and stuck a needle into the vein. I didn't feel it. Out of the corner of my eye, I saw Dr. Sherrill holding a pair of electric hair clippers. There was a loud click, and the clippers began to buzz. I realized they were moving toward my head.

"No!" I cried. "Please! Not my hair!"

The clippers slid across my scalp. I saw chunks of damp blond hair fall beside my table and onto the floor. An attendant prepared a soapy lather. She picked up a razor and walked toward me. She was going to shave my head!

The room began to spin. My stomach churned, and I felt faint. Then I heard a high-pitched noise, something between a buzz and a squeal. *It's a drill!* I was terrified. What were they going to do with it?

Someone held my head, and the drill began grinding into the side of my skull.

I began to feel drowsy. I was falling asleep, probably from the shot they had given me. I was glad I wouldn't have to listen to the drill anymore, but I was also frightened. *What if I don't wake up? Oh, God, I'm afraid!*

I saw faces. I heard voices. Nothing made sense. The room began to grow dark. The noise faded. I drifted into a deep, deep sleep.

3

Will I Walk Again?

Coming out of the darkness, I thought I heard the drill. I tried to open my eyes. I wanted to scream. I didn't want them drilling when I was awake. No words came. The room was spinning. I realized the noise wasn't the drill. It was an air conditioner.

I looked up at a ventilator grill above my head. I stared at the cracked, plaster ceiling. I tried to turn my head to see the rest of the room. Every time I tried to move, sharp pains bit into the sides of my head. Out of the corner of my eye, I could see large, metal tongs holding my head in place.

I lost consciousness again. I drifted in and out for days. My dreams were nightmares. I thought I was losing my mind. The next time I woke, I found myself face down. The tongs were still holding my head. I was enclosed in some sort of canvas frame with an opening for my face. All I could see was the floor right under my bed. Every two hours, two nurses or orderlies would come and "flip" me over. I'd spend two hours on my stomach, then two hours on my back.

I learned that the canvas bed was called a Stryker frame. It would keep me from getting the bed sores I was apt to develop because I couldn't get out of bed.

I was in the hospital's intensive care unit or ICU. The hours blurred into days. I got to know my roommates better.

Tom was a young man who was there because of a diving accident, too. It was funny. I knew Tom had broken his neck, but I didn't understand that I had broken mine. Nobody had told me.

With the nurses and our family visitors acting as note takers and couriers, Tom and I began to send messages to one another.

Tom was in worse shape than I was. He couldn't even breathe on his own. He had a respirator that breathed for him. I found the sound of that machine comforting. As long as I heard it, I knew Tom was okay.

One night, the sound stopped. I choked as I tried to call for help. I heard the nurses rush into the room. "His resuscitator is down!" one of them yelled. "Get a new one, stat!"

I heard footsteps running down the tile hallway. I heard the metallic sounds of the oxygen unit being removed. Someone at the nurses' station called for emergency help. The room was full of people.

"Tom! Can you hear me, Tom!" a doctor called. "Where's that other resuscitator?" he snapped.

"The orderly had to go downstairs for another unit," a nurse explained. "He's on his way."

"Keep up the mouth-to-mouth. We've got to keep him alive until ..."

I lay there staring at the ceiling. Even if I could move, there was nothing I could do.

I heard the elevator doors down the hall open. I heard footsteps running toward the ICU ward. Someone said, "I've got a unit. You want me to make room?"

I was horrified at the reply. "Never mind," the doctor said. "We've lost him. He's dead."

I felt the flesh on the back of my neck crawl. They were talking about Tom. *Tom was dead.* I grieved for Tom, and I was more afraid to go to sleep than ever. I was afraid that I would die, too.

These fears were pushed to the back of my mind during visits from my family and friends. They came to see me as often as they could. It made me feel bad when I was facedown in my Stryker frame

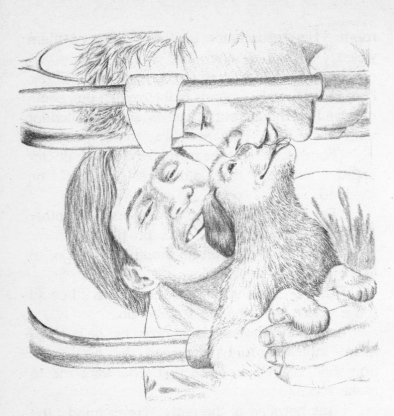

and they had to get down on the floor to talk to me. It was the only way that I could see them.

One day in August, my boyfriend, Dick, came in wearing a jacket. The day was sunny and warm, and I wondered what he was up to.

"I—I've just run up all nine floors!" he gasped.

I laughed. "Why didn't you use the elevator?"

Dick got down on the floor, under my Stryker frame. "This is why." He opened his jacket and pulled out a small, lively puppy. It began to climb all over Dick. It licked his face. "Yip, yip, yip!" the dog barked.

"Shhh. Quiet, pooch," Dick begged. "You want us to get kicked out of here?"

He put the puppy up to my face. I felt its fuzzy warmth. Its wet tongue licked my cheek. It was a wonderful surprise. "Oh, Dickie—he's beautiful. I'm glad you brought him."

We were startled when a nurse walked into the room. "I thought I heard something in here," she said.

"You aren't going to turn us in, are you?" Dick asked her.

She grinned. "Who me?" She bent down and cuddled the puppy. Then she put him back down on Dick's chest. "I don't see a thing." Still grinning, she left the room.

Dick and I played with the puppy for nearly an hour. I was sorry when they had to go. He picked up the dog. "I'll take the stairs again," he said as he got up to leave. "Otherwise they may search me every time I come up here!" He left with the puppy hidden under his jacket.

The next day I had a bone scan and myelogram done. The bone scan was like taking a picture of my spine. The myelogram wasn't so simple. My spinal fluid was tapped and replaced with dye. When the tests were done, the dye was taken out and the spinal fluid injected back in. It was a very painful procedure. They had to keep me under sedation for several days.

When my doctor came by later to see how I was doing, I demanded, "Dr. Sherrill, what's wrong with me?"

"Don't you remember, Joni?" he said. "You have a lesion of the spinal cord caused by a fracture-dislocation."

I still wasn't sure what that meant. "You mean I broke my neck?" I asked.

"Yes."

When I was younger, I'd read the book *Black Beauty*. A man in the story fell from a horse and broke his neck. The man died. Tom had broken his neck. He had died, too. "But that means I'll die!" I said to Dr. Sherrill.

"No. Not necessarily," the doctor replied. "It means only that it is a very serious accident. The fact that you've survived four weeks now means you've more than likely passed the crisis. Many people don't survive accidents of this nature."

I thought of Tom again. "I guess I'm lucky," I said. I didn't feel very lucky, strapped in a Stryker frame, hurt and homesick.

"Lucky indeed," Dr. Sherrill agreed. "And strong. When you're strong enough, I want to perform fusion surgery."

"What's that?" I asked him. "In plain English."

"Your spinal cord is severed. We have to fuse the bones back together."

Back together! That meant he could fix my broken neck! That meant I'd get my arms and legs back. That meant, before long, I'd be back on my feet! It was the first good news I'd gotten since my accident. I couldn't wait for the surgery.

After the surgery, I was wheeled into a regular room instead of the ICU ward. *It's a sign that I'm getting better,* I thought. *If I wasn't, they'd keep me in ICU.*

Mom and Dad were waiting for me in my room. "Everything went fine," Dr. Sherrill told them. "The surgery was a complete success."

We all sighed our relief. "There will be difficult days ahead, Joni," Dr. Sherrill went on. "The toughest part will be in your mind. Wait until your friends go off to college. Wait until the novelty of this wears off. Wait until your friends get other interests and stop coming."

I didn't know why he was so worried. Now that the surgery had been successful, none of those things mattered. "I know it will take time, but I'll get better," I told him.

"How much time are we talking about, Dr. Sherrill?" my dad asked.

"Are you saying Joni won't be able to go off to college with her friends?" Mom wanted to know. "Should we wait until next semester?"

The doctor hesitated. "Uh . . . at least."

Mom was as surprised to hear it as I was. "Really?"

"Mrs. Eareckson," Dr. Sherrill told her, "I'm afraid college will be out of the question for Joni."

We still didn't understand what he was trying to tell us. "You mean that you don't know how soon Joni will walk again?" Mom asked.

Dr. Sherrill seemed surprised by the question. "Walk?" he said. "I'm afraid you don't understand, Mrs. Eareckson. Joni's injury is permanent. The fusion surgery didn't change that. We're hopeful that she'll be able to get the use of her hands back in time."

He glanced at me and then back at my parents. I was stunned by his words. Was I never going to walk again?

4

Why Go On?

I heard what Dr. Sherrill said, but I didn't want to believe it. I told my parents that Dr. Sherrill was wrong. I would get better and stronger. With God's help, I would walk out of the hospital.

But I didn't get better or stronger. The thought of food turned my stomach. I couldn't eat the meals they brought on my trays. My weight dropped, and I got weaker.

One day a stranger in a white uniform came into my room. "I'm Willie, the chef," he explained. "I came to see why you don't like my food."

"It isn't your food," I apologized. "I just get sick thinking about food in general."

"What did you like best? Before the accident?" he asked me.

I thought about it. "Before? Well, my favorite foods were steak and baked potatoes."

"Vegetable?" Willie asked me. He sounded like a waiter, taking an order.

"Oh, I don't know. Corn, I guess."

"Salad?" Willie demanded.

"I like Caesar salads," I told him.

"I'll see what we can do," Willie promised.

That evening when the nurse lifted the lid to my tray, I saw a big steak, a huge potato with butter and sour cream, sweet corn, and a magnificent Caesar salad. It looked wonderful. But when she set the tray down in front of me, the smell made me nauseous again.

"Please," I said. "Take it away. I'm sorry. I just can't eat it."

I couldn't eat, and I fought sleep because of the nightmares. My visitors were the one thing I looked forward to. One day, two girlfriends from high school came to visit. They hadn't seen me since the accident. They stared at the Stryker frame and all the equipment in the room. Then they stopped beside me. They didn't say anything.

"Hi." I smiled, trying to make them feel more at ease. "I'm sorry I can't turn my head to see you, but if you'll—"

"Oh, Joni!" One of the girls choked back her tears.

"Oh, my God," whispered the other.

They ran for the door. A few seconds later, I heard one girl retching and vomiting out in the hallway. Why had they reacted that way?

I was afraid to find out. It took a few days to work up the courage to ask my friend Jackie to bring me a mirror.

She looked up from the mail she was reading. "Why?"

The expression on her face made me more determined. "I want you to get me a mirror," I repeated.

She hesitated. "Uh . . . okay. I'll bring one next time I come."

What was she trying to hide? "No. I mean now. Get one from the nurse."

She tried to stall. "Why don't we wait. I'll bring your pretty dresser set from home."

I was getting angry. "Jackie! Bring me a mirror now!"

She left the room and returned with a mirror. Her hands were shaking when she held it up for me. I screamed, and Jackie nearly dropped the mirror. "It's ghastly!" I said.

It was worse than ghastly. The figure in the mirror was barely human. My eyes were darkened and sunk into their sockets, bloodshot and glassy. My teeth were black from my medication. My weight had dropped from 125 to 80 pounds. I looked like a skeleton covered by yellow, jaundiced skin. My shaved head only made it worse. No wonder my friends had run out of the room. I felt like vomiting, too. I burst into tears.

Jackie took away the mirror and began to cry with me. "I'm sorry, Joni. I didn't want you to see."

"Jackie, I can't take it anymore. I'm dying. Look at me. Why do they let me suffer like this?"

"I—I don't know, Joni."

"Jackie, you've got to help me," I begged. "They're keeping me alive. It's not right. I'm dying anyway. You've got to help me, Jackie."

"But how, Joni?" Jackie whispered.

"I don't know. Give me something. An overdose of pills. Or you could slit my wrist. I wouldn't even feel it."

Jackie's eyes widened. "You mean you want me to kill you?"

"Yes—I mean no." How could I explain? "You wouldn't be killing me. You'd just be helping me die sooner, Jackie. Can't you help me end the suffering? If I could move, I'd do it myself!" I was angry and frustrated.

Jackie began to sob. "I can't, Joni! I just can't."

After that, Jackie tried to help me look better when guests came. She tried everything she could think of to take my mind off my situation. "You'll be better soon, Joni," she promised. "Remember, the Lord says he will never allow us to suffer more than we can humanly bear."

I wasn't ready to hear it. I was angry. Why had God let this happen to me? Why did he let me suffer? "Oh, yeah?" I grunted.

The medication and paralysis made me more sensitive to light and sound than most people. I made Jackie and the nurses keep the shades drawn and the door shut to keep out light and noise. I could hear conversations from other rooms. The hospital routine grated on my ears.

One day, Jackie was moving a fan for me and accidentally dropped it. It sounded like an explosion going off in my head.

"Jackie!" I screamed and cursed at her. I called her awful names.

I felt terrible. I apologized the best I could. "Jackie, you're such a close friend. I take you for granted. I yell at you all the time. I feel like being mad at God, at Mom and Dad, at Dickie. It gets to me sometimes, and I have to let off steam. You're the only one I can scream at. Mom and Dad are already suffering so much. And I can't take a chance at losing Dick by taking things out on him. I'm sorry, Jackie. I've been taking it all out on you."

Jackie smiled. "That's okay, Joni. I know you don't mean it. Besides, what are friends for?"

Dick came by that night and talked about my accident being a test of faith. He told me that everything God does is for good. I didn't see how my being paralyzed could be for anybody's good. I decided that maybe, if I showed God I had more faith, he would help me get better.

The doctor told Dad our insurance wouldn't cover all our medical bills. "Don't worry, Dad," I said. "God will provide what we need."

Dr. Sherrill told me that paralysis is harder on an active, athletic person. "God will help me," I told him.

The physical therapist told me I had to get stronger so I could be transferred to Greenoaks Rehabilitation Hospital. "Oh, yeah," I said, trying to show my faith and confidence. "That's where I'll learn to walk again."

I spent nearly a month getting ready for the transfer. Three-and-a-half months after my accident, I was wheeled out to the ambulance that would take me to Greenoaks. A rush of sweet-smelling, outdoor air tickled my nose.

"Oh, wow! Wait just a minute, please," I asked the orderlies. "Do you smell that air?" I'd almost forgotten what it was like.

One of them laughed. "Yeah," he said. "It's polluted."

I breathed deeply. Polluted or not, I thought it was wonderful. "Oh, it's beautiful!"

I enjoyed the ride to Greenoaks, drinking in the sights and sounds of the city. When I took my first ambulance ride, the trees had been green. The air had been hot and humid. Now the air was crisp and cool. The stores we passed were decorated for Halloween. The trees were gold, red, and orange. A whole season had passed since my accident.

I tried not to think about the time I'd lost. I let the warm sun bathe my face through the window and pictured Greenoaks in my mind. A big, colonial building with tall, white pillars. Sweeping green lawns shaded by huge green oak trees.

We pulled into the driveway. Greenoaks Rehabilitation Hospital looked more like a factory. "Anything wrong?" the driver asked me.

I did my best to hide my disappointment. "Uh ... no, I guess not." I stared at the run-down, low, brick building.

"Don't worry," the driver told me. "They do good work here. I think you'll like it. Quite a few girls your age are here. You should hit it off well."

I wasn't so sure about Greenoaks. I wasn't so sure about anything anymore. "I hope so," I said.

5

Dark Days at Greenoaks

Mom and Dad were waiting for me in my room. Their smiles were stiff. Their eyes tense. They didn't stay long. They had reacted the same way when Dr. Sherrill told me I wouldn't walk again. I knew they were as disappointed with Greenoaks as I was. I knew they didn't want me to see them cry.

Greenoaks was nothing like I had imagined it. It was an old, dilapidated building. The halls were dark and depressing. I saw people slouched in wheelchairs. People in Stryker frames. People lined up in wheelchairs. I didn't see anybody who was walking, anybody who was healed.

Four other girls shared my ward. At least it would be good to have some company. "Hi. I'm Joni Eareckson," I introduced myself.

"Joni Eareckson!" Somebody swore. "That's all I heard at City Hospital. Joni this. Joni that. I could puke!"

I was surprised by the bitter anger in the voice. "I didn't know I had a fan club here," I said.

The other girls laughed. "You'll have to excuse Ann," one of them told me. "She's new here, too. She came to City Hospital after you did. I guess she wasn't the model patient you were. I'm B.J. The girl in the bed over there is Denise."

"Pardon me if I don't get up," Denise said.

"Yeah," I joked back. "I know the un-feeling."

"And this is Betty," B.J. pointed with a flop of a useless arm.

B.J. had a broken neck like I did. Betty had a blood clot on her spine. Denise had multiple sclerosis.

"How long have you been here?" I asked B.J.

"Two years."

Two years! B.J. was still paralyzed and in bed like me. I didn't want to think about being here that long. I tried to pray that night, but I couldn't.

My days were all the same. I had to stay in bed because of bedsores. A nurse would feed me in the morning and empty my catheter bag. Then she'd adjust the round mirror over my head so I could watch TV.

About noon, I'd be fed and "emptied" again. Then I'd watch more TV in the afternoon. In the evening came another meal and catheter emptying and more television until lights out. All I did was eat, sleep, and watch TV. I had to learn to eat and drink quickly. The staff was always busy. They had other people to feed and other things to do.

One day my sister Jay came to visit. "What's that horrible smell?" she asked.

I hardly noticed the hospital smells anymore. "What smell?" I said.

"Ugh! It's your hair!" Jay wrinkled up her nose. "When did they wash it last?"

"Over a month ago at City Hospital," I told her.

"It's awful. It stinks! I've got to do something about that." Jay got a basin and soap and figured out a way to shampoo my hair.

"Oh, it feels so good!" I exclaimed.

"Me next!" called out Denise. "Wash my hair, too, Jay. Please?"

"Me too!" Betty and B.J. said at the same time.

So Jay washed, set, and brushed our hair for us every week until hospital regulations put an end to it.

I was glad when Physical Therapy, or P.T., became part of my daily routine. At first, the therapist came to my room to exercise my paralyzed arms and legs. After a few weeks, I was taken to the P.T. center for two hours a day.

The P.T. center reminded me of a torture chamber in an old horror movie. There were all sorts of strange machines for stretching, bending, and pulling useless arms and legs. But I was sure that the P.T. center was where I would learn to walk like the other patients I saw moving with crutches and walkers. I didn't realize how hard it would be just to learn to sit up again.

First the staff members fastened me to a tilt-board. Then they slowly raised my head and lowered my legs. I felt the blood rush from my head. Waves of nausea swept over me.

"Wait. Don't go any higher. I can't take it," I cried. After nearly six months in a horizontal position, even a few seconds with my head up was too much for me. Another disappointment.

"Oh, Joe," I sobbed to the therapist. "Will I ever be able to sit up?"

"Sure, Joni. It just takes time. We'll try again for a little bit longer. When you can take it for several minutes, we'll raise your head higher. By Thanksgiving, you should be sitting up in a chair."

We worked longer and longer each day. Finally, I could sit up on the tilt-board without blacking out or getting sick to my stomach.

Diana White, a friend from school and Young Life, started coming by regularly. She was always cheerful. She always had a word of encouragement from the Bible. One day she read John 16:23: "I assure you that whatever you ask the Father he will give you in my name."

"Isn't that great?" Diana asked me.

"Yeah, it really is." I told her about the prayer service they were having for me at our church and the tingling sensation I'd felt in my fingers during P.T. I knew God was beginning to heal me.

Joni's Story

But the morning after the prayer service, I didn't wake up healed. I told myself the healing would come in a slow and natural way. I hid my disappointment when family and friends came to visit.

"Oh, Joni," someone would gush. "You are so brave. I wish I had your faith."

I'd smile sweetly and pray under my breath for God to hurry up and heal me.

By December I was still weak, thin, and covered with bedsores. But my physical therapy had given me enough sitting up time that I could go home for one day. The choice was easy. Wearing the new blond wig Jay had given me, I went home for Christmas.

The house was decorated for the holidays. A big pine tree and a hospital bed were set up in the family dining room. The sights, sounds, and smells were almost too much for me. I half sat, half lay on the bed.

"Please, will you cover me, Mom?" I asked.

"Are you cold, dear?"

"No. I just want to be covered. I look awful."

Mom and Jay told me I looked lovely, but I insisted. I didn't want people staring at my useless legs. I didn't want to see them myself. They reminded me how different this Christmas was. No shopping for presents. No caroling. No sled riding. No going to church with the family. I enjoyed the time with Dick, my family, and my friends. But I was sad, knowing how much my life had changed.

When I got back to the hospital, they told me it would be my last visit home for a while. The sitting up had opened the sores on my back and hips where my bones protruded through the skin. I would have to go back to a Stryker frame until they healed.

Dick hitchhiked the sixty miles from the University of Maryland as often as he could. He always tried to lift my spirits and build my faith. I knew it was hard on him. I knew it had hurt his grades. When his grades went down, he even lost his football scholarship. I loved seeing Dick—being with him. But I knew I wasn't being fair.

"We're holding onto the past, Dickie," I told him. "We can't go back to our high school days."

"Things will get better," he insisted.

"No!" I cried. "I'll never get better. Can't you see that?"

Things only seemed to get worse. My sores, caused by my protruding bones, did not heal. The doctors insisted that surgery was the only way to correct the problem. On June 1, I was taken back to City Hospital for the bone operations.

The surgeon, Dr. Southfield, explained the surgery. "Since you have no feeling, it won't be necessary to put you to sleep. But if you're squeamish about the sight of blood...."

"Never mind," I said curtly. "I've been here almost a year, remember. There isn't much I haven't seen. And there isn't much they haven't done to me. Carve away!"

I listened as Dr. Southfield guided the scalpel through the flesh on my hips. The blood spurted as he laid back the skin and muscle tissue. I heard a strange rasping sound as he chiseled away on my hip bone, filing down the sharp joints that caused my bedsores.

In spite of my brave talk, I didn't like the sounds. The sight of blood made me queasy. I began to sing to take my mind off the operation. I sang loud and long, every depressing song I knew.

"Can't you sing something else, something brighter?" Dr. Southfield asked.

"No!" I snapped. How could he expect me to go through something like this—wide awake—and be cheerful too? I kept up my concert until I was turned over and Dr. Southfield began to operate on my tailbone. Finally, he sutured all the incisions. I was bandaged and taken back to Greenoaks.

When the sutures and bedsores healed, the orderly placed me in bed and tried to help me sit up. "How about that, Earl!" I told him. "I'm sitting up!" It felt so good.

Earl didn't answer. He carried me back to the Stryker frame.

Dark Days at Greenoaks

"Hey, leave me in bed," I told him. "I've waited so long to sit up again. I'm not going to pass out."

"Sorry, Joni," Earl said softly. "I gotta put you back in bed. Your operation didn't take. Your backbone just busted the incision open again. You're bleeding."

6

A Reason to Trust

Back in my Stryker frame, I finally gave up all hope of ever walking again. I began to concentrate on getting back the use of my hands. If I had my hands, I could do things for myself. I could brush my own hair. I could put on makeup. I wouldn't have to depend on Jay and Diana so much. I wouldn't feel so helpless.

"You can use your mouth to do some of the things you used to do with your hands," my occupational therapist Chris Brown suggested. "You've seen other people writing or typing with a pencil or stick in their mouths. You could do it too."

It would be like giving up hope of using my hands again. "No!" I told her. "It's disgusting. Degrading. I won't do it!"

Dick and Diana would come to read the Bible with me. I didn't see how what they read applied to me. How could my being paralyzed work for good? I shut out the messages of hope and trust. What sort of hope did I have strapped into my Stryker frame? How could I trust God after all I'd been through?

Some of the people at Greenoaks made me feel even more helpless. Mrs. Barber, one of the night attendants, acted like the patients were a bother instead of people needing care and concern. She was mean and insulting when nobody else was around. I was afraid of her.

One night she came into our room and angrily swept my pictures off the window air conditioner near my Stryker. She swore at me. "How do you think I can turn on this air conditioner with all this stuff on it?" she hissed. Then she picked up a picture of Dick and said horrible things about him.

When I snapped back at her, she came over to my Stryker and snarled, "I ought to leave you like this until morning and not flip you at all." She gave me a mean smile. "But to show you what a nice person I am, I'll turn you."

She knew she wasn't supposed to turn me by herself. Without checking to see if my arms were tucked in, she flipped me violently. I had no way to protect myself. One of my arms was loose, and my hand hit against the Stryker frame.

Since I was paralyzed, I didn't feel any pain. But

my hand swelled up and was badly bruised. Mrs. Barber didn't even look at it. She left my injured hand dangling down and went out the door.

I began to cry.

"I saw what she did, Joni," B.J. told me. "You ought to report her to the supervisor."

"Yeah," Denise added. "I heard everything. You ought to turn her in."

"I can't report her," I sobbed. "She'll do something else. Something worse."

The next day, Mom came to visit, and she asked me about my hand. I tried to make believe it had been an accident, but the other girls told Mom what had happened. She went right to the supervisor and complained.

Late that night, Mrs. Barber came into our darkened room. She tiptoed up to my frame and put her face next to mine. "If you ever say anything against me again," she whispered, "I'll see that you pay for it dearly." I was terrified.

Not everyone was like Mrs. Barber, but even the staff who did care were so overworked that they didn't have time to do more than provide basic care. It made me feel more helpless and hopeless than ever.

Like most of my high school friends, Diana had gone off to college. One day she told me she had decided to drop out for a semester or two. She wanted to become a volunteer at the hospital so she could take better care of me. "I've prayed a lot about it, Joni," she said. "I believe it's what God wants me to do."

Diana thought it would be a good idea for me to learn to write with my mouth.

"But I'm making progress in physical therapy," I protested. "Why should I learn to write with my mouth? I'm going to get back my hands."

"What if you don't get your hands back, Joni?" Diana asked me.

I didn't want to think about that. Diana kept telling me I should trust in God. Why would God keep me in a wheelchair and take away my hands too? It didn't make sense.

"Maybe you should take it one step at a time," Diana suggested.

I decided she was right. I was in a rehab hospital. I should start working at getting rehabilitated. The next day I told Chris Brown that I wanted to learn how to do things by using my mouth.

"What do I do, Chris?" I asked her.

"Hold this pencil in your mouth. Grip it with your teeth, like this." She held a pencil in her own mouth to demonstrate. Then she put one in my mouth, and I bit down on it.

"Not so tight, Joni," Chris said. "You'll get writer's cramp—in your jaw. Just hold it tight enough to control it. See?"

"Mm—mff," I mumbled.

First I learned to make lines, then circles and other marks. At first the lines were squiggly and wobbly. After hours of practice, I had more control. It was like being in kindergarten again. Finally, I was able to make letters. Concentrating as hard as I could, I wrote a letter to Mom and Dad. It was short. It took me a long time to do it, and the letters were still big and squiggly. But I was writing!

In September, I was taken to Kernans Hospital for another back operation. My protruding backbone made it impossible for the bedsores on my back and bottom to heal. The hospital was only a mile from our house in Woodlawn. It was hard to be so close, knowing I wasn't ready to go home.

This time the operation was a success. But I still had to spend fifteen days lying face down in a Stryker frame. To pass the time, I did a lot of reading, especially reading the Bible.

October 15 was my birthday. One of the best presents I got was being turned face up again. Dick and my family came to visit me. Things began to look brighter. Since the operation was a success, I could start looking forward to using a wheelchair. Some of my paralyzed friends at Greenoaks had been sent home. This gave me more hope, something to look forward to. I worked even harder at my own therapy. I wanted to go home, too.

I was ready to try new things. "Now that you can write pretty well with your mouth, why not do something artistic?" Chris Brown suggested.

"Artistic?" I asked. I wasn't sure what she had in mind.

"You've shown me the drawings you used to do. You can paint these ceramic discs. They make nice gifts."

I watched one of the other quadriplegics slop paint on a piece of clay using a paint brush she held in her mouth. It reminded me of kindergarten again.

"I—I don't know," I said quietly.

"Oh, come on. Try it," Chris urged.

I tried the painting, spilling globs of color, splashing clumsy designs on the clay discs. It was discouraging and frustrating. And messy. At first, I hated every minute of it.

When the discs came out of the kiln, they didn't look so bad. I was encouraged. I practiced. And I improved. After a few weeks, I had Christmas gifts for my family and friends. I didn't know what they'd think of the candy dishes, but I thought they were pretty good, considering. And I had done them myself!

One day, Chris brought me some moist clay.

"What's that for?" I asked.

"I want you to draw a picture on it," she told me.

"How? With a pencil in my mouth?"

She shook her head. "Try this stylus." She showed me a long wooden stick, pointed at one end.

"What should I make? Should I write something?"

Chris smiled. "Why not make something that *you* like," she suggested. "Something to express yourself."

I gauged the distance from my mouth to the clay and poked at it with the pointed end of the stick. Then I tried to etch something.

The last time I'd drawn anything was on our

trip West, just before my accident. I had filled a sketch pad with drawings of mountains, horses, people, and animals. I tried to remember how to draw.

I looked down at the sketch I'd done: a line drawing of a cowboy and horse etched in the soft clay. It wasn't very impressive, but it was a beginning.

Chris was amazed by my first attempt. "Joni! That's great. You've got real talent." She grinned. "You should have done this before. You have to get back to your art."

"That was when I had hands," I protested.

Chris shook her head. "Hands are just tools, Joni. The skill, the talent is in your brain. Once you've practiced, you'll be able to do as well with your mouth as you did with your hands."

"Wow! Really?"

"Yeah," Chris said. "Want to try it?"

It turned out to be a very satisfying day for me. For the first time in almost a year and a half, I was able to express myself in a creative, productive way. It was another reason to hope.

And it was a reason to trust. I began to believe that God understood. That there was some plan behind all that had happened to me. I began to sign "PTL" on my drawings: Praise The Lord. I knew God cared for me.

7

Beginning Again

I improved and grew stronger. In early December, Mom and Dad told me about a new hospital they'd heard about.

"It's called Rancho Los Amigos," Dad told me. "It's in Los Angeles."

"They've been able to teach people to regain the use of their arms and legs," Mom added. "Even so-called hopeless cases."

It sounded like the answer to my prayers. "Oh, wow!" I exclaimed. "Let's go there. Can we?"

"I think it looks good," Dad said. "We can't go with you, but Jay wants to go. She can rent an apartment nearby to be with you."

I might be going to California! To a place

where I could learn to use my hands again. "Wouldn't that be some Christmas present?" I said.

It was an exciting Christmas. I hadn't been home for a whole year. This time I was strong enough to stay for several days. And when Dick asked me to go with him to a movie, I was really thrilled. "It will be like the old days," I told him.

As much as I wanted to be normal again, to have a date like any other couple, it was impossible. When Dick put his arm around me, I didn't even know it. He squeezed me affectionately, but I couldn't feel a thing.

"Don't you feel that?" he asked.

"What?"

"This." He squeezed me again.

"No," I said softly. I was embarrassed. "I—I'm sorry." I really wanted to feel his arm, his touch.

Driving home later, Dick was forced to stop suddenly. I flew forward and hit my head on the dash. I couldn't stop myself. I couldn't even pick myself up. I wasn't hurt, but my pride had been injured.

Dick was really upset. "Why didn't I remember to hold onto you?" he asked.

"Dick, please don't blame yourself. It takes some getting used to. And I'm not hurt. Let's not let it spoil our evening."

We drove home, and Dick wheeled me into the house. "Thank you, Dickie," I said. "I really had fun.

This is the first time I've done anything normal in a year and a half."

"It was a lot of fun," Dick said. He leaned down and kissed me on the forehead. "Glad you enjoyed it."

It was fun. But it wasn't really like the old times. I wondered if things would ever be normal again.

When Christmas was over, I didn't want to go back to Greenoaks.

"You don't have to, Joni," Dad told me.

"What?"

"Rancho Los Amigos has room for you. We'll be leaving next week. After New Year's."

I began to cry. "Oh, Daddy. I'm so happy. The Lord does answer prayer."

Rancho Los Amigos, I said to myself. *That's where I would get back my hands.*

I didn't try to guess what Rancho Los Amigos might look like. I had been too disappointed when I first saw Greenoaks. But Rancho turned out to be beautiful. Many of the orderlies and staff people were college students working their way through school. I was glad to have people my own age to talk to. My therapy started right away.

I couldn't bend my fingers or my wrists. I couldn't pick up a spoon or a fork. But I learned to raise and lower my arms by using my back and shoulder muscles. Then a special spoon was attached to my arm brace. By moving my arm, I could swing it into a plate of food, scoop up a bite, and lift it back toward my mouth.

I had fed myself without having to think about it for seventeen years. Now it took all my concentration. I felt like a steam shovel, and sometimes I spilled more than I got into my mouth. But it was still exciting. I was actually feeding myself.

My doctor was pleased by my progress. And he didn't send my friends Dick and Diana away when they drove all the way to California to visit me.

"I want them to come," he said. "As often as they can."

"Really?" I was surprised. The other hospitals had always been so worried about regulations.

"Yes. I want them to learn about you and your handicap. Then they can help take care of you when you go home."

I hadn't really thought about going home for good. "H—home?" I stammered.

"I think you should plan to finish here by April 15," the doctor told me.

I couldn't believe it. "But that's only three months!" I said. "Will I be ready?"

"That's up to you. Are you willing to work at it?"

"Oh, wow!" I told him. "Am I!"

One of the first things I worked at was using a wheelchair by myself. Judy, one of the attendants, showed me how to make it move by throwing my arms against the knobs on the wheels.

"I want you to drive to P.T." she told me.

"But I don't have P.T. until nine o'clock," I told her. "It's only seven now."

Judy just grinned. "Right."

It took me the whole two hours to go thirty feet down the hall to the physical therapy room. By the time I got there, I had no strength left for my exercises. Judy was waiting for me.

"Beautiful!" she said.

"Does everybody take this long?" I asked her.

Judy nodded. "Especially the first time. A lot of them just give up. Some of them even fall out of their chairs."

I felt proud. For the first time in over eighteen months, I had moved myself where I wanted to go. And I hadn't fallen out of the chair, either!

I practiced "driving." Sometimes I veered into a wall and was stuck for thirty or forty minutes until someone rescued me. Finally, I was given an electric wheelchair to use. I got so good at it, I practically lived in my chair. After so many months in bed, it was good to be able to get around on my own. I even got to go out by myself.

The neighborhood around the hospital had special ramps and sidewalks built for wheelchair travel. It gave me a feeling of independence to be able to go over to the Taco Bell and order fast food for the other patients, even if the man at the counter had to take the money out of my wallet to pay for the order.

"I think I'll enter you in the Ontario 500," he teased.

I didn't enter the Ontario 500, but I did like to race in my wheelchair. Rick, another quadriplegic who had been into sports, did too.

"I can make my chair go faster than yours," I bragged one day.

"Oh, yeah?" he said. There was no mistaking the challenging gleam in his eyes.

There was a whirring sound as our chairs raced down the corridor in a fifty-yard dash. It was a tie.

"We can't get up any speed here," Rick said. "We have to go farther. Let's race from this corner of the building all the way to the other end of the hall, around the corner, to the front doors."

"You're on!" I said.

Judy and another attendant pretended not to notice and walked the other way.

"On your mark!" I called to Rick. "Get set. Go!"

We were off side by side, veering noisily down the hall.

"Don't crowd me, Eareckson." Rick laughed. "Get over to your own side of the street!"

Patients in their rooms stared or smiled at us as we raced by. First Rick's chair pulled into the

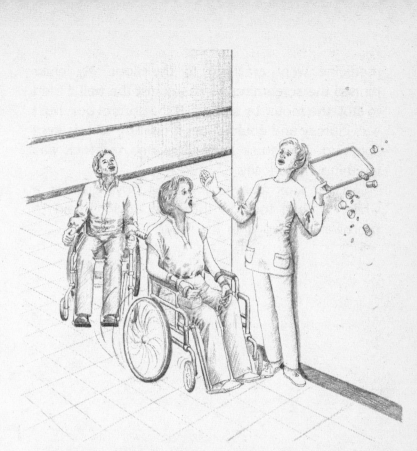

lead. Then mine. Then his again. Neck and neck, we went into the far turn.

I was determined to win this time. I swung into the corridor without slowing down. As I whipped around the corner, I came face to face with a nurse carrying a tray full of bottles and medicine. I don't know who was more surprised—she or I.

She froze. I screamed, "Look out!"

Too late. The tray went flying. Bottles and

medicine went crashing to the floor. My chair pinned the screaming nurse against the wall. I tried to stop the motor by striking at the control box, but I was clumsy and couldn't get it off. The wheels kept spinning. The nurse kept shrieking. And Rick was laughing hysterically.

They took away my driving privileges for a while. When I took to the road again, I had to promise to keep it in low gear.

8

Snap Out of It!

By April 15, 1969, I had reached my goal in rehab, and they told me I could go home. I was pleased by the progress I had made, but I still had a big question in my mind. A question I was afraid to ask.

"Doctor, I've been working hard to get my hands back. Now I'm beginning to wonder if I ever will."

"No, Joni," the doctor said bluntly. "You will never get your hands back. You might as well get used to the idea."

It was the opposite of what I had been hoping, praying to hear. How could I get used to being dependent and helpless forever? The reality of my injury began to sink in slowly. I would be a quadriplegic *as long as I lived.*

I wrote Dick and told him the news. It was one of the hardest things I'd ever done. In part of the letter, I wrote:

> I can never be a wife. I know you love me as I love you. God must have something else in mind for us. Let's go on being friends, Dickie. But I want you to be free to date other girls and look for God to lead you to the right one to marry. I can never be that woman.

I signed it "Joni" instead of "Your Joni" the way I used to do.

On the outside, I was happy when I got to go home again. On the inside, I was bitter and angry. God hadn't answered my prayers. He hadn't given me back my hands.

Diana spent a lot of time taking care of me. She tried to encourage me. "You can't give up, Joni," she told me.

"Why not?" I demanded.

"You've got to work with what you have left," she said.

"I have nothing left."

"Don't give me that," Diana scolded. "I saw people at Greenoaks and Rancho who were really bad off—blind, mute, deaf. Some even lost their minds. *They* have nothing left, Joni. But you have your mind, your voice, your eyes, your ears. You have everything you need."

"We'll see," I said.

Dick came to visit. He tried to get me to change my mind about breaking it off between us. "Joni, I don't care if you get healed. I want to marry you anyway."

"It wouldn't work," I told him. "My paralysis is almost too much for me to handle, let alone you."

"Sharing the burden would make it lighter for both of us," Dick said.

"That's romantic," I told him. "But it isn't very realistic."

Finally he agreed with me. "Maybe you're right," he admitted. His eyes filled with tears. "Maybe I can't deal with it."

I couldn't deal with it either. I began to spend a lot of time sleeping and daydreaming. I spent all my time thinking about the way things used to be. Memories of the good times, the fun I'd had. When friends came out to our family farm to ride, I'd think about all the times I'd gone riding. When I sat by a friend's swimming pool, I daydreamed about when I used to go swimming.

It was Diana who helped me snap out of it. "Joni! Stop it! Wake up!" she screamed one day. She took me by the shoulders and shook me.

"Wh—what?"

"Joni! What's wrong?" Diana asked. "Are you

sick? I was talking to you, and you were just staring into space."

"Leave me alone!" I told her. "Just leave me alone."

"It isn't going to help you to avoid reality," Diana said. "You've got to face up to the truth. The past is dead, Joni. You're alive."

"Am I?" I challenged. I couldn't walk. I couldn't use my hands. Most of my body was numb. What could I do with a life like that? "This isn't living."

Diana wouldn't let me give up or feel sorry for myself. She'd scold me back from my fantasy world whenever she caught me daydreaming. As soon as I could, I drifted off again. Taking a nap in a dark room with the air conditioner humming in the background worked best. I spent my time in a dream world, living in the past. I avoided the present and tried not to think about the future.

Finally, I realized that I wasn't getting anywhere. I decided my attitude was sinful. I began to pray that God would help me understand his will for me. "Do something in my life to help me serve you and know your Word," I prayed.

The answer wasn't quite what I expected. "I'm going to bring a friend over to meet you," Diana . said not long afterward.

"Who? Why?"

"Steve Estes. He has a love for the Lord and a real knowledge of the Scriptures. He's a young guy. In fact, he's still in high school."

"High school! Diana! He's a kid?"

She smiled. "Wait till you meet him."

I didn't have long to wait. He came over that evening, and the minute he walked through the door—tall, dark-haired, green-eyed—he shattered all my preconceived notions about him.

The first thing I noticed about Steve was his attitude toward me. Many people who meet me for the first time seem awkward and uncomfortable because of my wheelchair. Usually, I feel self-conscious. But Steve was completely at ease. He made me feel comfortable, too.

We started studying the Bible together. I realized that I had to forget the past and concentrate on the present. It was hard, but I got rid of as many reminders of the past as I could. I gave away my hockey and lacrosse sticks. I even sold my horse, Tumbleweed. I knew she would be better off with someone who could give her the attention and exercise she needed. And I started putting my trust in God.

Steve asked me to talk about my faith to the youth group at his church. The thought of speaking to fifteen teenagers terrified me. I didn't do very well. I stammered and hesitated. My throat went dry. My face turned red. My mind went blank. Somehow Steve picked up on what I'd said, and we got through the evening.

Afterward I told him, "I never want to do that again as long as I live!"

"All you need is a little experience," Steve said. "Maybe you should go to college."

I hadn't thought about going to college for a long time. Hadn't one of the doctors told me it was out of the question?

"You could go to classes in your wheelchair at the University of Maryland," Steve went on. "They have quite a few handicapped people there. You shouldn't have any trouble."

"Maybe you're right." Hadn't I said myself that it was time to put my trust in God and get on with my life?

Steve nodded and gave me a wide grin.

"All right," I told him. "If Jay and Diana will help, I'll go to college this fall."

In September I began taking a few classes in public speaking. My speeches were about things I knew and could discuss easily—relating to people with handicaps, accepting the wheelchair, and my Christian experience.

When I saw that people were interested in what I had to say, I became more confident. I was asked to work as a counselor for a local Young Life club. I even went to the Young Life summer camp in the Colorado Rockies. I was growing in faith and trust. And, deep inside, I knew that God was preparing me for something.

9

Something Better

In the fall of 1970, I met Donald Bertolli, a friend of Dick's.

Donald was a handsome man with large, dark brown eyes. He worked with Baltimore street kids. After our Young Life leadership meeting, he asked if he could see me again.

"Sure," I told him. "Come over any time."

He showed up at our door the next morning.

I was still in bed. Jay came in and woke me. "Someone's here to see you," she said. "I don't know who he is, but he's sure good-looking. He says his name is Don."

He ended up staying for lunch—and for dinner. "Can I come back to see you?" he asked before he went home.

"Uh . . . well," I hesitated. I was afraid he'd be on my doorstep bright and early the next morning. "I have classes tomorrow."

"I'll take you," Donald offered.

"Uh . . . thanks, but Jay usually takes me. She knows my routine."

"Well," he said. "I really enjoyed the visit. Let's do it again."

"I'd like that," I told him.

He met us the next day after school and spent the rest of the day with us. At first, I thought he was sort of pushy. By the third day, I was beginning to like him.

We saw a lot of each other that summer. Donald even took me to Ocean City. He stood beside my wheelchair on the boardwalk. I enjoyed the fresh, salty ocean air and the sounds of sea gulls and crashing waves.

I sighed, thinking about how it used to be. The feel of the sand between my toes. The cool water splashing over me in the surf.

I was surprised when Donald began pushing me off the boardwalk into the sand. He didn't stop when we came to the water. He plunged ahead until I was out in the water, up to my legs.

"Donald! What are you doing!" I screamed. The people on the shore stared at us, as if they were wondering what this man was doing to that poor girl in the wheelchair. I laughed as Donald picked

me up and carried me out into the breakers. I couldn't feel it, but I knew my heart was pounding madly.

That was one of the things that made Donald special. He made me feel "normal" for the first time since my accident. The wheelchair didn't get in his way. He didn't pity me or feel uncomfortable around me. He treated me as he would any woman he liked.

Summer turned to fall. We went on trail hikes. When he'd pushed the chair as far as he could, he'd fold it up and carry me the rest of the way. He'd spread out a blanket, and we'd have a picnic lunch and enjoy the scenery.

I enjoyed it, but I was worried about my growing affection for Donald. Many of my friends had gotten married. I had even been a bridesmaid in a couple weddings. But I had given up thinking about either getting married myself or having a boyfriend. How could I?

Donald said he loved me. He talked about getting married and taking care of me. But my friends warned me to be careful. They didn't want me to be hurt.

Donald and I began to pray that I would be healed. There was even a special healing service at our church. Our prayers were not answered. I began to accept the fact that I would never be healed. Donald and I stopped talking about our future together.

One day he came and told me he was taking a new job, working at a Young Life camp in New York. "I'm sorry, Joni," he told me. "It's over." He wasn't really trying to hurt me. It was just his straightforward way of handling things. He turned and walked to the door.

"Donald! Don't leave me, Donald," I begged.

"Good-bye, Joni." He closed the door behind him.

"Why, God?" I asked him. "Why are you hurting me like this?"

It was hard for me to accept the fact that Donald was not God's will for me. I trusted that he had someone, something better in mind. I didn't know what it might be. But God knew.

Over the lonely summer, I turned back to my art. And it seemed my art was getting better. I gave drawings to friends as Christmas and wedding presents. They noticed the difference, too.

I didn't want people to like my drawings just because I was in a wheelchair and drew with a pencil in my mouth. I wanted them to think my art was good. I tried different kinds of paper and pencils. I began to feel that my art had something to do with God's will for me.

One day, an insurance executive named Neill Miller called on my Dad in his office. He noticed one of my drawings on the wall.

"I really like that drawing," he told Dad. "Is it an original?"

"Yes," Dad said. "As a matter of fact, my daughter Joni drew it."

"Really? She's quite an artist. It shows great discipline."

"You might be interested to know," Dad went

on, "my daughter is paralyzed. She has to draw holding the pen in her mouth."

Mr. Miller examined the picture more closely. "Amazing. Has she exhibited her work anywhere?"

"Just a couple of festivals," Dad told him. "She does it for fun. For friends and family."

"Do you think she'd mind if I arranged a small exhibit for her?" Mr. Miller asked.

"I'm sure she'd be delighted," Dad said.

The "small" exhibit was arranged at a local restaurant. Jay, Diana, and I drove down together. When we turned the corner, we found that the street was closed.

"That's strange," I said. "Why would they block off a main street?"

"Maybe it's a Lincoln's birthday parade," Jay guessed.

"Yeah," I said. "It must be a parade. Look."

"A brass band!" Jay said. "Too bad we're going to the exhibit, or we could watch it."

"Maybe we could cut down—" I didn't finish. We all gasped at once. The brass band was in front of the Town and Country Restaurant. A huge banner across the front of the building announced: "Joni Eareckson Day." A television crew and a crowd of people were waiting for us.

I wanted to run, to hide. We had no choice but to go ahead. I prayed that Jay wouldn't drop me as she and Mr. Miller lifted me from the car into my wheelchair.

"Mr. Miller," I whispered. "What have you done?"

Before he could answer, I was surrounded by reporters. I was given a big bouquet of flowers. An official from city hall read a proclamation from the mayor announcing Local Art Appreciation Week and Joni Eareckson Day. I was pleased when the reporters asked me more about my art than my wheelchair. I was even more pleased when people seemed to like my work and bought my paintings.

Mr. Miller introduced me to a handsome young man. He had his hands stuffed into the pockets of his coat, and he looked uncomfortable. "I wanted him to talk to you, Joni," Mr. Miller said without explaining why. He left us alone, staring at one another.

The young man sat down next to me. I tried to make conversation. "What do you do?" I asked him.

"Nothing," he said. "I used to be a fireman. But I can't work now."

"Oh?" I didn't know what to say. "Will you tell me about it?"

"It was an accident."

"Yes?" I still didn't know what his problem was.

"Look," he said. "Miller said I should talk with you. He said you had a rough time a while back . . . with your . . . handicap."

"I sure did," I admitted. "I was really depressed. I think I might have killed myself if I could have used my arms."

The young man's handsome face twisted with pain. He pulled his own arms out of his coat pockets. He had no hands. Just scarred stumps where his hands used to be.

"My hands were burned in a fire," he told me. "And I just can't cope." His voice broke.

I understood how he felt. I told him about my experiences in the hospital and at Greenoaks. I told him his feelings were natural. I told him how God had been working in my life.

We talked for half an hour. When he left, he said, "Thanks, Joni. Neill Miller was right. You have helped me. I'll try again."

The art exhibit came to an end. I had sold a thousand dollars worth of my drawings at fifty to seventy-five dollars each. I was asked to appear on a local talk show. A major newspaper did a feature article about me.

I was invited to participate in local art shows. I was asked to talk to Christian women's clubs, schools, and church groups where I showed my artwork and talked about God. I even had a special tour of the White House. I got contracts for other television and radio appearances. It felt good to be able to earn my own money and begin to support myself. It felt good to be able to share God's promise of hope and love with so many people.

I created a line of greeting cards and started my own company, Joni PTL. I even became a partner in a new Christian bookstore. Then, in the summer of 1974, I was asked to come to New York City. I was going to be interviewed by Barbara Walters on *Today*.

After the show, Jay told me, "Just think, Joni. You probably talked to twenty or thirty million people this morning about your faith!"

Not long before, I had been too nervous to talk to fifteen teenagers in a small, local church. Now I'd traveled to New York City and shared my faith with millions of people on national television.

After the program, I got invitations to do more speaking and more radio and television interviews. Paper Mate, the company that made the Flair pens I used in my drawings, arranged a series of national exhibits. Articles and stories appeared in several magazines. An editor from Zondervan Publishing House called and asked me if I'd be interested in writing a book about my experiences.

I had no writing experience. I couldn't imagine writing a book, even with a professional writer like Joe Musser to help me. "My friends and family might read it," I said, "but I don't think anybody else would be interested."

The book turned out to be a best-seller. It was

translated into more than thirty languages and read by millions of individuals. People from all over the world wrote me letters to tell me how much my book had touched their lives.

Amazing things had happened when I put my faith in God. I began to wonder what else God had planned for me.

10

Making the Movie

World Wide Pictures decided to make a movie of my book *Joni*. They asked me to play myself. I knew it would be hard to relive the accident and the time I'd spent in the hospital. But I thought the movie would be a good way to share my message of God's grace and love with more people. I thought it would mean more to people if they saw the real me instead of some actress.

We started with the diving scene. They got a girl who looked just like me to act out what happened right before the accident. I watched her swim out to the raft, pull herself out of the water, then dive back in. Then it was my turn.

"Okay, we're ready for Joni!" Jim Collier, the director, called.

Two paramedics put me on a rubber raft and floated me out into the shallow bay. I floated on my back and waited for the cast and crew to get into position. Everyone got quiet. I took a deep breath, and Jim signaled for the paramedics to flip me over, face down in the water.

I heard Jim shout, "Action!"

The actress playing my sister Kathy splashed through the water, calling my name. The bay was cold and dark. My lungs were hungry for air. I almost shook my head to signal to the paramedics that I needed help. The actress playing Kathy lifted me out of the water. I sputtered and gasped for breath. It didn't take a lot of acting.

Most people think that making a movie is really glamorous and exciting. But things didn't always go as planned. One day we were shooting the scene where Dick sneaked the puppy into my room. I was anxious to get it over with. I had to lie in a Stryker frame for the hospital scenes. The canvas straps hurt my forehead and chin.

Cooper, the actor playing my boyfriend Dick, pulled the puppy out of his jacket. He said his lines. "Here, pup. Lick Joni's face."

The puppy wouldn't cooperate. It whined and squirmed to be let loose.

"Cut!" Jim ordered.

We tried the scene a second time. And a third. After the fourth take, they brought in a new puppy.

The new puppy wouldn't lick my face either. He wouldn't have anything to do with me. The crew laughed. Face down in my Stryker frame, I didn't feel much like laughing.

Four puppies and fifteen takes later, I agreed to let the puppy handler smear liver-flavored baby food on my cheek.

"Action!" Jim called.

The puppy wiggled and squirmed in Cooper's hand. He caught a whiff of the liver and furiously licked my cheek. The camera caught the action. The crew cheered. The scene was finished at last.

Another time, Cooper and I had to do a kissing scene. When Dick used to come to the hospital to see me, there was no place we could be alone. So we'd hide in an elevator and flip the button so it would stop between floors. That was the scene Cooper and I had to act out.

I was nervous doing a kissing scene in front of a movie crew with an actor I hardly knew. Cooper was very nice and very handsome, but I didn't really know him. It had been a long time since I'd been kissed by a boy. I decided to take no chances. Alone in my bed that night, I practiced the best kisses I could remember—on my wrist.

We went to a hospital to shoot the scene. The elevator was rigged with stage lights, microphones, and electric cables. There was hardly any room left

for Cooper and me. I was pushed into one corner of
the elevator. Jim pulled Cooper in next to me.

Cooper sat on my lap. Jim yelled, "Action!"
Cooper leaned forward and kissed me. I forgot all
about the lights and camera.

"Cut!" Jim yelled.

Laughing, Cooper patted my hand. "Boy, you
kiss good," he said.

"Okay, let's do it again," Jim told us.

Again Cooper leaned toward me. We kissed a little longer than we had to.

"Hey!" Jim yelled. "We don't need another cut, you two!" Everyone laughed.

One day we went out to Rancho Los Amigos to film some of the rehab scenes. I met a young boy who was sitting rigid and upright in a body cast. A metal halo was bolted into his skull, keeping his neck still as it healed. He could move his arm a little. He was working on painting clay discs while we talked about making the movie. It reminded me of my own therapy at Rancho.

Afterward, one of the Rancho staff, Debbie Stone, told me more about the boy in the halo cast. "His parents don't want anything to do with him," she said.

I couldn't believe it. You needed your family most at a time like this. "Why?" I asked Debbie.

"He broke his neck in a motorcycle accident. Driving while he was drunk." Debbie shook her head. "They figure he got himself into this mess, so he can get himself out."

I wished that I had said more to the boy. I wished there was some way I could help him.

"Joni, you wouldn't believe the problems most handicapped people face," Debbie said. "Spiritual struggles, yes. But down to earth, practical problems too."

I realized that Debbie, disabled by polio and in

a wheelchair herself, was doing what I would really like to do. Helping people in the real world to see Christ.

I thought I knew what God wanted me to do next with my life. In the spring of 1979, I moved to California to begin my ministry with the handicapped. We started Joni and Friends.

11

Almost Like Getting Healed

You know, it's not too late to change your mind," Jay told me as we packed the pickup truck full of my belongings.

Jay was more than my sister. She had been my nurse, my roommate, and my friend. I would miss her. And I knew she would miss me. Leaving would be hard.

"I believe this is the right choice," I told her.

I kept remembering my conversation with Debbie Stone at Rancho Los Amigos Hospital. "Joni, you wouldn't believe the problems most handicapped people face. Spiritual struggles, yes. But down to earth problems, too."

I was a handicapped person who had experienced God's overwhelming love and grace. I had a loving family and friends who had cared for me. There were thousands of people who had none of that. I knew I had to help them. Los Angeles seemed like a good place to start.

I had made a lot of good friends while I was making the movie. The people at Grace Community Church even arranged for me to use a small house nearby. Judy Butler and my cousin Kerbe would be living there with me. Not long after we moved in, I went to see Dr. Sam Britten at the Center for Achievement for the Physically Disabled.

The center reminded me of Rancho Los Amigos, but I noticed one big difference. Weights slammed. Straps buckled. People worked at their exercises. They chatted, and they laughed. It was the laughter that made the difference.

Dr. Sam asked me if I'd like to learn to drive.

"Everybody knows I don't have the muscles to turn a steering wheel," I told him. I had been tested by many doctors. They had all agreed that I could never learn to drive.

Dr. Sam looked into my eyes. "You can do it," he said. "I know you can. We'll worry about the steering wheel later."

A few minutes later I was working a cycling machine, moving the pedals with my arms. I hadn't done any hard, physical exercise for a long time.

Remembering my lacrosse and hockey days, I breathed deeply. I stretched and challenged my muscles. It felt good.

Puffing and panting, I was glad when Dr. Sam came over and told me I had done enough for one day. "I'll design an exercise program for you," he said. "You'll be on the freeway in no time."

I laughed, thinking about myself driving down the freeways in one of the special vans I'd seen parked out front. It was a good thing Dr. Sam had never seen me racing a wheelchair.

The congregation of Dr. Sam's church surprised me with a new, cream-colored van to help with my ministry. Sam said it was just an example of what churches could do to help the handicapped. He said it would help me get my message and God's Word to more people. Of course, I'd have to learn to drive it first.

A special lift raised and lowered me into the van. The front seat had been taken out so I could sit in my wheelchair instead. There were push-button controls so I could start the motor with a jab of a mouthstick. And my hand fit into a special cuff that controlled the speed, brakes, and steering.

The van was ready, but I wasn't sure I was. "I can't believe I'm doing this," I told Sam as I inched the van out of the parking lot. I drove down the back streets, avoiding the main roads. Teeth clenched, I braced myself for the stop sign up ahead. I flexed my bicep, pulling back on the joystick. The van jerked to a halt. I was still several yards from the stop sign.

"Stay calm, everybody," I said, trying to stay calm myself. "I have every move carefully planned." After a while I relaxed. I breathed deeply and began to glance at the houses that flowed by. A few months ago, I wouldn't have believed it was possible, but I was driving! Just like everybody else.

After a few more days on the road, I was convinced that I could drive—even on the freeways. All I had to do was convince the people at the Department of Motor Vehicles to give me a driver's license. Rana, a friend from the Achievement Center, drove down with me.

I told myself this was crazy. I grinned, imagining what the other people in line must be thinking. I couldn't even lift a glass of water to my mouth, and here I was about to tell these people that they should let me on the road.

Finally, it was our turn at the window. The woman behind the counter looked at Rana instead of me. I cleared my throat. "Good morning," I said. "I'm here to take the written exam for drivers. I can't use my hands, but my friend here can—"

The woman didn't let me finish. "May I have your learner's permit, please?"

I tried to continue. "As I was saying, I can't write

with my hands, but my friend here can help me take the exam."

The woman thumbed through some papers on her counter. "I'm sorry," she said to her paperwork. "You'll have to come back next Friday morning a little earlier. Handicapped people may only take the oral exam with one of our employees in the conference room. The room is closed now."

Rana and I looked at each other. It had taken a

mountain of effort to get me ready this early. Why should I have to come back? "We're not leaving until I take this exam," I whispered to Rana.

I smiled and cleared my throat again. "I'm a mouth artist, and I hold brushes and pencils between my teeth." The woman's eyes widened. "If my friend is allowed to hold the test on a clipboard, I can take it that way."

The woman went to talk to her supervisor. In a few minutes, she came back. The woman still talked to Rana instead of me, as if I couldn't think for myself just because I was in a wheelchair. "I think she'll be too much of a distraction to the other people taking the exam. Do you know what I mean?"

Rana turned to me. "Do you know what she means?"

I would not be put off by this woman and her red tape. "Well," I said, a tinge of anger in my voice, "how about this. Let's tape a pen to my wrist. If you don't mind my straying out of the little true and false boxes a bit, I can take the exam that way."

The woman left to talk to her supervisor again. She finally returned with a roll of masking tape and led us to the examination room. I was very pleased with myself until I saw the desks. They were made so that people could stand up and take the test. I couldn't reach them from my chair.

Rana and I came up with a solution. She put a

waste basket upside down on my lap and propped the exam paper on top where I could reach it.

"Frankly," I told the woman. "I think I'm far more of a distraction this way!"

I passed the written exam and the road test, though the examiner was so fascinated that I could drive at all, he kept forgetting to tell me where to turn and when to park.

I had my driver's license! I could drive to meet someone for dinner. I could drive myself to work at Joni and Friends. I could drive to watch a sunset. Even more wonderful, I could drive alone. For the first time in the fifteen years since my accident, I could actually go somewhere—anywhere—by myself!

It was almost like getting healed.

12

Lessons in Friendship

One day, Dr. Sam asked me if I would talk to some of his students.

"Yes, of course," I said. Talking to these people about the struggles I'd faced—dealing with pity and stares, learning how to live on my own and yet depend on others, and seeing God's part in all of it—was what my ministry was all about.

Everyone seemed to listen. Everyone except a beautiful young woman with dark, curly hair. Her name was Vicky Olivas. Later, someone told me her story.

Vicky had gone to a factory looking for a job.

Instead of hiring her, the man at the factory attacked her. He shot her in the neck with a gun. She had tried going to a psychologist. She had tried being hypnotized. She had even traveled all the way to Russia to a special treatment center. Nothing helped. She was still paralyzed. She was living on her own with only a part-time, paid attendant and her five-year-old son to care for her.

The more I heard about Vicky, the more I wanted to be her friend. I wanted to help her accept and trust the Lord. I just wasn't sure how to go about it.

I tried inviting her out to dinner. When we talked about her son, Arturo, everything was fine. Vicky was even willing to talk a little about herself. When I tried to talk to her about God, she said it was time to go home.

I asked Rana what went wrong. "I don't know how to put this," she said. "But you can't just waltz into her life and act like you have an easy answer for all her problems. You don't."

I had been thinking of Vicky as a project, not a person. I asked myself what Jesus would have done and what I could do to help Vicky. Then I thought of something I had experienced when I was making a record album.

After I made the movie *Joni,* some people at a record company asked me if I'd like to make an album. I was bowled over that they thought my singing was good enough to put on a record. And I was thrilled that I'd have a new and exciting way to share my faith with others.

A time was set for the recording session. When I went to the studio, I was surprised to find a whole orchestra—violins, cellos, horns, trumpets. The music and voice tracks were recorded separately. First the orchestra recorded the music. Then I sang the words to what they'd recorded. It was exciting to sit there and listen while they played.

As soon as they finished, the musicians walked away. Some of them went outside to chat. Some went for coffee. None of them stayed to listen to the playback of the music. I couldn't believe they didn't want to stay and hear the beautiful music they'd created, to know how it had all turned out. They acted as if it wasn't that big a deal, as if they didn't care.

"Hey!" I wanted to shout. "God listens. *He* cares!"

That was the message I wanted to share with Vicky Olivas. No matter what happens, you can always lean on God. God is never too busy to listen. He cares. I wanted to find some way to show her that I cared, too.

I started by offering her one of my extra corsets. "It helps me breathe and sit up," I told her. "It's the only reason I can sing or even talk loudly."

Rana and Judy lifted Vicky onto the bed and

rolled her body to position the corset under her middle. She grunted and puffed as they tugged at the straps and fastened the buckles.

"I'll bet you feel like an old packhorse," I told her. "I always do."

Back in her wheelchair, Vicky fought to gain her balance. "This isn't easy," she said. Then she smiled. "Oh, my goodness! What a difference this makes in my voice."

We spent the afternoon talking. I shared some of the hints I'd gathered from my many years in a wheelchair. And I offered her my extra easel so she could start to learn to write with a pen between her teeth, the way I had.

"Maybe we could show your attendant how to put the corset on and—"

Vicky sighed. "My last attendant left. Thank goodness."

"What do you mean?" I asked her. I had never been without family or friends to take care of me.

Vicky hesitated. "We got into this argument. She got so angry, she took a pillow and she put it on top of—" She looked up, her eyes filled with tears. "On top of my face. She was so mad, she wanted to kill me."

The room was silent. "Luckily," Vicky went on, "my brother was upstairs. He ran down the steps when he heard me scream. He grabbed her by the hair and threw her out the door and told her never to come back."

Vicky sniffed. "I need someone. Anyone. Arturo is just a little boy. He and I can't go on alone this way."

"Let's start by praying," Rana suggested softly.

Vicky's answer startled us. "Jesus can't help me. It isn't Jesus who can put me to bed or get me up in the morning," she told us. "He can't get me a drink of water. It's nice that you all believe in God, but I need somebody more . . . more real than God. I need people."

"I need them too, Vicky," I said. "The only difference is that I know that Kerbe and Judy and others are like . . . like the hands of God for me. It *is* Jesus who gets me up in the morning. He just uses people to do the work that needs to be done."

"Has one of your people ever tried to murder you?" Vicky asked me. I didn't know what to say about that.

We were still looking for an answer to Vicky's problem several days later. Judy, Rana, and I had gone out to dinner. We talked about it over our dessert.

"What was it that helped *you* the most?" Judy asked me.

"My situation was so different," I told her. "My family's unusually close. And I've got great friends."

Like Vicky said, it was people who could make the difference.

Judy grinned. "Well?"

I wasn't sure what she was getting at. "Well, what? Do I stick you two in a copying machine and pass out copies?" I wished I could. So many people, like Vicky, needed help.

"Sort of," Judy said. "Why don't you train others to help like we do?"

Rana agreed. "Look at all those people in churches on Sundays. Some of them must have some free time."

"You mean we should have a class or something?" I asked. "Teach people how to push a wheelchair or whatever?"

"Yeah," Rana said. "And maybe they'll even learn to empty a leg bag. I've always heard that Christians should set a good example. We're supposed to care about people in need, right?"

Excited about the idea, we used the backs of our napkins to jot down our plans. Before long, we had planned our first "People Plus" workshop. More than a hundred people came: college students, mothers, teachers, nurses, and businessmen. It was another good beginning. A beginning of the volunteer training, family camps, Bible studies, daily radio programs, and all the outreach programs that are part of Joni and Friends today.

Not long after our first "People Plus" workshop, I had to spend two months in bed. All my speaking, traveling, driving, workshops, and painting had taken their toll. I had been sitting up too many hours a day. The old pressure sore from my movie days was now an open, oozing wound.

After my accident, God had given me the grace to endure more than two years in the hospital. Now it was hard for me. I was used to being active and on the go, getting out and doing things. I read the Bible, but it wasn't easy. I was lying on my side. The book had to be propped up on its end with a pillow. The words were hard to read sideways. And it was impossible to turn the pages. I spent a lot of time eating and watching television. The rest of the time I just lay there, getting more and more depressed.

Vicky and Rana came to see me. "How's the sore?" Vicky asked.

"Oh, it's coming along," I told her. "How have you been?"

"Fine," she said. "I got a new attendant." It was good to see her smile. "It's working out great."

She talked about her new helper, about studying the Bible with Rana, about Arturo, and about the new van she was getting. I talked about how boring it was to be stuck in bed, how behind I was in my painting, and how many speaking engagements I had to cancel. I stopped, annoyed at myself for whining and complaining so much.

"Sorry," I apologized. "I'm not very together right now."

Vicky smiled. "I guess the tables are turned."

I was puzzled. "What do you mean?"

She told me how she used to think I had it all together when I first started coming to Dr. Sam's center. "You had a house, a van. You had your work at Joni and Friends. You wrote a book. Even if you were a quad, your problems were nothing compared to mine. Then I felt ashamed when you wanted to be my friend. I didn't know why you'd want to. I guess it was just envy."

I knew what she meant. Sometimes it's hard not to envy people who seem to have it easier than we do. "Sometimes I look at paraplegics and think they've got it made because they can use their hands and don't have to depend so much on other people," I admitted.

"Do you really do that?" Vicky asked.

I nodded sheepishly.

"I do too." She laughed, and I laughed with her.

Our injuries were very similar. Our lives were very different. We were friends. "If we trust God, we can make it through anything," Vicky told me. "Together."

13

Enter, Ken Tada

It was Friday night. I could hear the buzz of Kerbe's dryer in the bathroom.

"Got a date?" I yelled above the whine of the dryer.

"Yes. A potluck dinner at church."

I wheeled up to the bathroom door and watched Kerbe teasing and pulling at her hair. I laughed. "You look like a lioness."

Kerbe threatened to paint a mustache on me with her blue eye pencil. Ready to go at last, she pulled a spray bottle out of her purse. "You want some perfume?" she asked me.

"I'm not going anywhere," I told her.

"That's not the point." Kerbe squirted the scent

on my neck. Long after she left, I could smell the perfume in the air.

My thoughts strayed back to the long-ago days when I was on my feet, getting ready for my own Friday night dates. I sighed. I couldn't even remember my last date. I chuckled to myself. Guys weren't exactly beating down my door to take me out.

It was a weekend like most weekends. Grocery shopping. Sales at the mall. A few hours of painting. A phone call home to my family. An early night on Saturday. Church on Sunday.

The sermon got a little long, and as hard as I tried to concentrate, my mind began to wander. My eyes settled on a dark head down in front, four or five pews ahead. Since I couldn't seem to take my eyes off the dark-haired man, I decided to pray for him. After church, I almost went over and introduced myself. "He'll think I'm crazy," I told myself. I forgot all about it.

A month later, a friend came up to me after church and introduced me to a nice-looking oriental man. He looked vaguely familiar. Then it came to me. "Turn around," I told him. "I want to see the back of your head."

He looked puzzled and gave me a funny sort of a grin, but he did what I asked. Sure enough, he was the man with the thick, black hair. I told him I'd prayed for the back of his head a few weeks ago. He laughed. We talked for a few minutes, and I asked him his name.

"Ken Tada." He smiled.

I kept running into Ken Tada after that. At church. At a Young Life meeting where I was the speaker. My friends tried a little matchmaking. They invited Ken to my birthday party, even though I hardly knew him.

I liked what I saw of him, though. He seemed comfortable with himself and with other people. He looked people in the eye when he talked to them. And he smiled a lot.

He came over at the end of the party to say good night. He leaned against the wall beside my chair, and we chatted. I found out that he taught social studies at a nearby high school and coached football.

Finally, I said I should go. I had a long drive home by myself.

"How about if we continue this conversation over dinner next Friday?" Ken asked me.

"I suppose so," I replied. "Sure, I'd like to."

The next morning, a bouquet of roses was delivered to my house. "For me?" I asked Kerbe. "Who are they from?"

Kerbe took the card out of its envelope and read me the note. "Looking forward to Friday. Ken Tada."

Friday evening, Ken arrived promptly and with

more flowers. He wheeled me out to his car. He took off his jacket and rolled up his sleeves. Then he squatted by my chair to lift me. With a mighty karate "hi-yah!" he heaved me to his chest. I felt *very* heavy.

"You really aren't heavy at all," Ken told me as he backed the car out of the driveway. "Light as a feather."

I remembered his mighty hi-yah. "Oh, really?" I said. "I never would have known."

"Well, I have been working out," Ken told me. "Lifting weights."

"How much weight did you train with?" I asked him.

"Oh, about 175 pounds."

I was astonished. "A hundred and what?"

"I wanted to be sure I didn't drop you," he said. I wasn't sure if he was joking.

We drove to a restaurant called The Warehouse. There was no wheelchair ramp.

Ken wheeled me back to the bottom step, tilted me back, and pulled me up one step at a time. "Easy," he said.

He seemed comfortable with me. Cutting my shrimp. Giving me a bite of his appetizer, a drink of water. He made me feel very comfortable too.

"You've been around disabled people, haven't you?" I scooped up another bite of shrimp.

"Well, yes and no." Ken told me about his work

with the Special Olympics. "But dating someone in a wheelchair—no." He leaned back in his chair and shook his head. "I've never done that before."

"Well . . ." I grinned. "There's something else you're going to have to do that you've never done before."

"What's that?" Ken asked.

"My leg bag needs emptying."

"Okay," he said. "Just tell me what to do."

He paid the check and wheeled me to the restrooms. We paused in the hallway. We stared first at the ladies' room on the right, then at the men's room on the left.

"Uh," Ken said, "I think we have a problem here."

"Yes, well," I teased. "I hadn't thought about this one."

People were walking around us, going in and out of the restrooms. "Come on, Joni," Ken whispered. "What should I do?"

"I think we should head outside and find a tree," I told him.

A few months later, Ken took me to Disneyland.

"Let's try that wild roller coaster on the other side of the park," I told him. "I think we can handle it."

"Great, let's go!" Ken plopped his Mickey Mouse ears on my head and unloaded an armful of

popcorn and drinks in my lap. "We'll really have to move, though. The lines to that thing are blocks long."

"Ah, but I've got a secret!" I told him.

He followed behind my chair as I pushed through the thick lines snaking their way to the ride entrance. "What do you think you're doing?" he asked me. "We can't just cut in front like this!"

"I'm not going to cut in front," I told him. "I'm

going to cut in back." I led the way to the exit where an attendant swung the gate wide open to let us in. "See?" I asked Ken.

Ken and the attendant lifted me into the waiting bobsled. The boy buckled me in while Ken lowered himself in behind me. A car slammed into the back of our sled. Ken gripped me with his arms as the toboggan lurched forward.

"I'm not ready! I'm not ready!" I yelled.

Our sled started slowly up the first steep incline. "Am I in?" I asked Ken.

"Yes, you're in!" Ken yelled back.

Our sled plunged down the crest. "Hold me! Hold me!" I yelled. My body slammed from one side of the sled to the other. "I don't have any balance."

Ken let go of the handholds and pulled my body against his. With no way to hold on, both of our bodies slammed against the side as the sled jerked around a corner. Ken giggled hysterically.

"I think . . . I think I'm going to die!" I yelled.

It seemed to take forever for the sled to come to a halt in front of the exit again. The attendant laughed when he saw the two of us lying flat at the bottom of the sled. "We let disabled people ride twice if they want," he said. "Saves the hassle of getting in and out again."

"You're kidding!" I told him. "What are you guys trying to do, get rid of us?"

"Hey, let's do it, Joni!" Ken laughed with glee,

scooting himself up behind me again. A car slammed into ours and jolted us forward.

"Hey! No way!" I said emphatically. "Not again!"

More cars hit us from behind and propelled us down the tracks. "Too late!" Ken laughed.

Afterward, by the exit, we stopped to catch our breath, puffing and wheezing. I flung my arm against Ken. "I could have been killed!" I told him. I was laughing too.

Later, at dinner, Ken said, "Being disabled has its advantages. No standing in lines. Going in exits. Riding twice. Even the parking places are bigger." He took my hand. "Knowing you is a real plus, Joni—in more ways than one."

Knowing him turned out to be a plus for me too. Two years later, Ken Tada and I were married. It was the beginning of another chapter in my life and his as we learned to put our faith in God and strive to do his will together.

14

A World of Difference

Look at these children!" I told Ken. The pictures in *World Vision* magazine wrenched my heart. I knew that in the United States disabled people like Vicky Olivas had it bad. But in countries overseas, like the Philippines or Nigeria or India, it was much worse. "They don't even have wheelchairs to sit in."

There had to be a way to help. When some Filipino churches heard about Joni and Friends, they asked us to come over and speak to them. I wanted to do more than sit in my wheelchair in front of a crowd of disabled people. I wanted to do more than talk. I wanted to offer practical help.

We asked some friends connected with our ministry to help us raise money for wheelchairs for the handicapped people in the Philippines. When we got there, we invited disabled people to come and get the chairs we had brought with us. We lined the chairs up in front of a hospital. On each chair was a copy of my book *Joni* and a Bible in the Filipino language.

I cried as the people came forward to get their chairs. Some of the handicapped children had been carried to the meeting on their fathers' backs. Some of the disabled men and women had been brought up on folding chairs or straw mats. I realized how much I had to be thankful for. God had given me so many things.

God also gave Ken and me a way to share his Word and his love by extending the ministry of Joni and Friends to people in more than twenty countries, all over the world. The need—and the lessons and the love—are the same wherever we go.

In Poland, I met a young man sitting in an old wheelchair, its drab-green leather cracked and torn. The wheels were different sizes, and the mismatched armrests were taken from other, even older chairs. Yet this man's chair was better than many of the others I saw.

Our message in Poland was about trusting and obeying God. It was a lesson Ken and I have learned together, through our lives and through our marriage and ministry. I talked to the people, mostly farmers, about their horses, obediently plowing the straight and narrow, plodding under a heavy yoke.

In Hungary, we traveled from city to city, sharing our stories and talking with people in churches, hospitals, and rehab centers. Some of their wheelchairs were made out of spare bicycle parts and pieces of plumbing pipe. But they came, and they listened, and they shared their faith and love with us.

After the last meeting in Hungary, a little girl pushed through the crowd. It was hot, and I was tired. The little girl reached the side of my wheel-chair. There were tears in her eyes as she shoved a tiny, handmade, terry cloth rabbit into my lap. She jabbered something in Hungarian, gave me a huge hug around the neck, and ran back into the crowd.

As Ken kept pushing me forward, I searched the crowd for the little girl. I wanted to find her and thank her. I love stuffed rabbits and have collected them ever since I was a little girl. Her gift meant a lot to me.

I never found her. I never got to tell her thank you. But I still take "Rabbie," the terry cloth rabbit she gave me, whenever I travel. When I go to a hotel, we unpack Rabbie and prop him up on the table by the bed. He's a reminder for me to pray for all the children around the world, especially the disabled children who need our help, our love, and our prayers so much.

I'm an artist; I draw and paint. I write books for both children and adults. I've made a movie. I've recorded albums. I have a radio show and a ministry with Joni and Friends that lets me travel all over the world talking about Jesus. But these are not the things that make my mark in eternity. Jesus asks the same thing of me that he asks of you. We must both learn to trust and obey.

One hot July day, a lifetime ago, I dived into the cold, murky waters of the Chesapeake Bay. When they pulled me from the water, I was paralyzed. I thought my life was over. I thought I would never be happy again. I didn't see how God could possibly use my paralysis for good.

But *God* knew. Maybe his idea of good for me didn't mean getting back the use of my hands or legs. But His idea of good meant a big change in my attitude and in the way I look at what's important in life. God's idea of good also meant reaching out to others like Vicky, and the disabled people I met through JONI AND FRIENDS, and many others around the world.

Yes, there are times when it's still hard living in my wheelchair. But I'm always learning to put my life in His hands and my trust in Him. And that makes all the difference in the world!

A World of Difference   *109*

Joni has formed an organization called JONI AND FRIENDS to encourage Christian ministry in the disability community.

If your mom or dad (or any other adult member of your family) would like to learn more about JONI AND FRIENDS and also receive information regarding her books, tapes, videos, and cassettes (many are for children), please have them write to:

JONI AND FRIENDS, Dept. Z
P.O. Box 3333
Agoura Hills, CA 91301